This book is especially for:

_____

You Can Call Me HOPPA!

The **Grandparents'** Guide to Choosing a Name that Fits

BY LAUREN CHARPIO

To Gramme, Hoppa, Gramma and PawPaw with love and admiration…

And to my husband, Casey: the patient, supportive, friend, dad, coach, chef, tickler monster, bug-catcher…

L.C.

Text Copyright ©2008 by Lauren Charpio

Book design by Darren Jones
Book edited by Paul Bradley

Printed in the United States of America

ISBN 978-0-615-19462-2

Library of Congress Cataloging – in – Publication Data Pending

They say genes skip generations. Maybe that's why grandparents find their grandchildren so likeable.
– Joan McIntosh

One of life's greatest mysteries is how the boy who wasn't good enough to marry your daughter can be the father of the smartest grandchild in the world.
– Jewish Proverb

Perfect love sometimes does not come till the first grandchild.
– Welsh Proverb

Table of Contents

Foreword

You Can Call me Hoppa! The Grandparents' Guide to Choosing a Name that Fits, was inspired by countless conversations between my husband and I, both of our parents and one important chance encounter. When we announced we were pregnant with our first child (the first grandchild for both of our sets of parents), it wasn't long before the discussion of 'what to be called?' arose among the grandparents. Both my husband and I had called our maternal grandmothers 'Nanny/Nannie.' Both of our mother's separately decided that they had no interest in taking that name – a decision that came as quite a surprise to both of us. They both independently expressed that the name Nanny would make them feel old. They wanted to think about grandparenting in a different way, a way that had not been actualized by their parents' generation. We went round-and-round for ages and never landed on anything that really felt like it 'fit' for either one of them.

My mother-in-law met a woman whose children lived in Hawaii and the grandchildren called her Tutu. She loved the name, but she knew that it didn't really fit for her. Ironically, both grandmothers-to-be decided that Grammie was the best of what they deemed to be limited options. This presented another conundrum – could they both really be called Grammie? Should one be Grammie P and the other be Grammie J? Should one of them choose another name? Who was going to be responsible for telling one of them they had to change it? Would our impending child get confused about these too-similar monikers?

As most things do, it worked itself out. My mom became Gramme, my mother-in-law became Gramma. But at the end of the day, neither of them were particularly thrilled with these titles. The grandfathers fared a bit better, which leads me to the genesis of this little book.

My father-in-law is from a long line of Cajuns and was born and raised in New Orleans. Because his cultural background was so important to him, he chose the traditional Cajun name for grandfathers, PawPaw. As it turned out, he was the only one with 'a name that fit' in those early days of 'what to be called?' discussions. My dad became Grandpa, and so it was for about 16 months… until the day our daughter began to try to say Grandpa. She would try to repeat just about anything we said – Grandpa was a tough one and when she finally took a shot at it, the result was HOPPA. We thought it was cute, but didn't make much of it for about a month or so. We had tried to correct her many times, until we finally decided that Hoppa was a much cuter name than Grandpa. By the time she was two, she could have pronounced Grandpa clearly and with ease but we wouldn't hear of it. He was Hoppa! Hoppa fit – it was original, sweet and genuine–just like my dad–and it now had a very special meaning because it was a name given to him by his granddaughter.

From then on, the name received a fair bit of attention. Friends and family love it and often express a bit of jealously at such a cute and fitting name. One friend of my dad's in particular was truly the inspiration for this book. I found myself in a business meeting with this long-time friend of our family, who has a son my age that was expecting his first child. This friend said that ever since a recent lunch with my dad, during which he discovered that my daughter called my dad Hoppa, he was on a quest for a grandparent name that was 'cool and hip' and didn't make him feel old. He told me that he had decided to be called The Bear! The next thing he told me was that he and my dad had discussed writing a book of grandparent names for the new generation, so that all of the newly crowned and up-and-coming grandparents wouldn't have to settle for a name that doesn't really fit.

After the angst and confusion my own family had experienced trying to avoid 'feeling old' while graciously accepting the title and role of grandparent, I then knew there might be grandparents everywhere who would jump at the chance to think differently about their moniker and I decided to write this book.

Introduction

The book is meant to be a fun thought starter and a bit of a keepsake.
We hope that you enjoy perusing the pages of possibilities, whether you
are a first-time grandparent or one who is relatively established. If you are a
first-time grandparent, our wish is to provide you with the inspiration to find
a name that really fits. Most of us are given a name at birth and don't again
get the opportunity to choose a name that truly represents who we are until
we reach grandparenthood.

If you are already a grandparent to young children and you are not thrilled with
your current title, we invite you to sit down with your grandchildren and ask them
to help you find the name that works for who you are. The name that is right for
you may not be contained within these pages, but we hope that we can provide
you with the inspiration you need to choose a name that fits!

*"**When I was a child** I called my grandmother **Nanny**. She was a telephone operator on Ellis Island and raised my mother as a single parent. She was beautiful and brave and smart, and I thought she walked on water. Growing up there was nothing I loved more than being told I looked just like her. When my son had his first child, I was so thrilled to be able to take the name Nanny in her honor. I only hope I can be as wonderful an influence on my grandchildren.*"

– Betsy R., Raleigh, NC

Traditional Titles

Many grandparent names are passed down from generation to generation, and a great number of these names hold tremendous meaning for families around the world. If your family has a rich heritage and you look forward to upholding tradition by taking the grandparent name that has been in your family for years, you will likely find that name in this collection of traditional titles. If you have special memories of your 'Grandmom' and the role she played in your life, you may feel it is important to honor her by taking the moniker yourself. This list has been compiled to pay homage to some of the traditional grandparent names that hold a special place in many of our hearts:

Grampy

Grandad

Granddaddy

Grandfather

Grandpa

Grandpapa

Grandpaw

Grandma

Grandmaw

Grandmama

Grandmom

Grandmommy

Grandmother

Granny

Granma

Granpa

Nana

Nanny/Nannie

Pa

Papa

"*When I was growing up*, *I had one set of Lebanese grandparents. My grandparents didn't use the Arabic names but my grandmother's sister was called Situ by her grandkids. I remember my Aunt Victoria and how much she loved the Arabic name- she enjoyed it when I would call her Situ, even though she was technically my Great Aunt.*"

– Jennifer H., Salt Lake City, UT

cultural Appellations

Respect, love and admiration for our grandparents is a truth shared around the world. Although titles may be different across cultures, we all speak these names with recognition of the experience and wisdom required to earn the important distinction of Grandparent. Many of our American families share a deep connection to their culture of origin. The German Oma, and Opa, the Italian Nonna and Nonno are uttered by children on playgrounds, in malls and at family gatherings around the country. This collection of cultural titles, both formal and familiar, may inspire you to choose a name that ties back to your cultural heritage.

Arabic - Sido

Arabic - Tae Tae

Arabic - Tata

Arabic - Gido

Cajun - PawPaw

Cajun - Mawmaw

Cherokee - Edudi

Cherokee - Elisi

Chinese - Ye Ye

Chinese - NaiNai

"**When I was a kid**, my mom was a French teacher. She thinks it is the most beautiful language and spoke it fluently, and tried to get us to do the same. When my sister had her baby, my mom was excited that she'd now be able to adopt the **French** grandparent name, **Memere**."

— **Christine R., San Francisco, CA**

"**I was born** and raised in a small village in **Greece** and left there only because I fell in love with a beautiful American woman. When our oldest daughter had her first baby it was so exciting — they gave him my name, Nicholas II, and I got to take the new name of **Pappou**! The two most wonderful things in the world!"

— **Nicholas A., Chicago, IL**

You Can Call Me HOPPA!

Danish - Bedstefar   Danish - Bedstemor
Dominican - Guelo   Dominican - Guela
Dutch - Grootvader   Dutch - Grootmoeder
French - Grand-père   French - Grand-mère
French - Pepere   French - Memere
German - Opa   German - Oma
German - Grossvater   German - Grossmutter
Greek - Pappous   Greek - Yia-yia

"My mother is called Tutu Helen. Tutu-kane is grandmother in Hawaiian and when our daughter was born, my sister lived in Hawaii. My mom wanted a cool grandma name so she requested Tutu and since it is really easy to pronounce, our daughter could say it early on and it stuck.

– Steve H., Salt Lake City, UT

Hawaiian - Tutu-wahini	Hawaiian - Tutu-kane
Hebrew - Saba	Hebrew - Savta
Hungarian - Nagyapa	Hungarian - Nagyanya
Hungarian - Apa	Hungarian - Anya
Icelandic - Ovi	Icelandic - Umi

You Can Call Me HOPPA!

> *My first son* was the first grandchild for my parents and so we knew that we would be setting the precedent for all future grandchildren. I knew even before he was born that he would call my dad "Granda." My dad is from **Ireland** and in English-speaking Ireland grandparents are referred to as **Granda** and Granny. Granda was easy, Granny did not fly and we came up with something else very cute for mom.

— **Megan F., Pittsburgh, PA**

Irish - Seanáthair
Irish - Daideó
Italian - Nonno
Japanese - Oji-chan
Korean - Halaboji

Irish - Morai
Irish - Maimeo
Italian - Nonna
Japanese -Oba-chan
Korean - Halmoni

"Growing up, I always referred to my **Norwegian** grandparents as *Bestemor* and *Bestefar.* When my son had his first child, my husband and I decided to alter the formal Norwegian names to something more fun. Now we're *Best-a-ma* and *Best-a-pa* and love it because we're always the 'Best' grandparents!"

— Hanna N., Minneapolis, MN

Norwegian - Bestefar	Norwegian - Bestemor
Philippino - Lolo	Philippino - Lola
Polish - Dziadzia	Polish - Babcia/Buscia
Polish - Zsa Zsa	Polish - Boo-Boo
Portugese - Avô	Portugese - Vovo
Russian - Dedushka	Russian - Babushka
Spanish - Abuelo	Spanish - Abuela
Spanish - Lito	Spanish - Lita

You Can Call Me HOPPA!

My parents are both originally from Stockholm, Sweden. *They are very proud of their heritage and we knew for sure that they would want to take* Swedish *grandparent names. In Sweden, the grandparent names are tied to your relationship with the grandchild. My mom is* MorMor *(Mother's mother) and my dad is MorFar (Mother's father). They absolutely love these names and they actually both got them put on their license plates!*

– Helena A., New York, NY

Swedish - Farfar   Swedish - Farmor
        father's father and father's mother
Swedish - Mormor   Swedish - Morfar
        mother's mother and mother's father
Turkish - Büyük Baba   Turkish - Büyük Anne
Ukranian - Dyido   Ukranian - Baba
Welsh - Tadgu   Welsh - Mamgu
Yiddish - Zeidy/Zayde   Yiddish - Bube

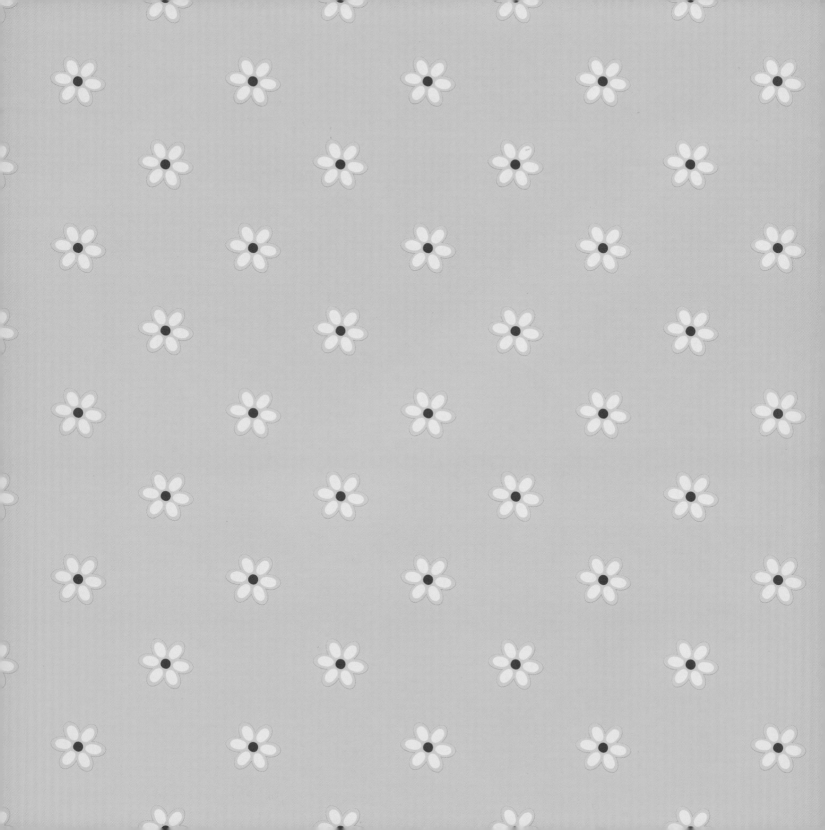

Perfectly Personal

Today's grandparents are diverse in composition; some have become grandparents at a young age, some at an older age and some have married into grandparenthood and have graciously accepted the role of Step-Grandparent. For many of these 'grands', names like Grandma and Grandaddy seem to either trigger perceptions of 'old-age' or suggest an approach toward grandparenting that is different from the approach they intend to take.

For these and a variety of other reasons, many may be hesitant to take on a traditional title and would much prefer something more personal that truly 'fits' who they are. For some it may be a nickname they've had since they were in school – the football team 'Captain' or the track star 'Wheels'.

For others, it may be a name that expresses their interests or hobbies; the basketball obsessed grandpa 'Hoops', or the gardener grandma 'Rosie'. Some may prefer something that highlights a signature physical feature; the bearded grandpa 'Beard-y' or the blue-eyed grandma 'Nanna Blue'.

If you are a grandparent, or grandparent-to-be, in search of a name that is 'Perfectly Personal', we hope this collection of titles inspires a name that fits for you:

Apple

"My maiden name is Smith and my mom thought it would be cute to be called Apple since she is technically a Granny Smith."

– Anonymous

Bear	Birdie
Be-Bop	Boss
Bella	Bubs
Big Daddy	Buba

You Can Call Me HOPPA!

Bogey

"My parents are fanatics about golf. My mom decided that being called Birdie would be a fun way to avoid a traditional grandparent name. It became a bit of a joke with my dad and because he's not quite as good a golfer, he became known as *Bogey!"*

– Ellen K., Furman, SC

Bubbe

Bud

Buddy

Buster

Butchy

Cat

Cha Cha

Chickie

Chief

"*My dad was adamant* about having a name other than Grandpa. He had been an executive for years and a few of his long-time colleagues called him *Chief*. He decided that Chief made him sound like he was in charge, which he thought would be important with grandchildren. The name stuck, but he's the biggest push over of all. "

– Emily P., San Francisco, CA

Coco	Dadoo
Contessa	Dandy
Cookie	De Dad
Cracker	Diva

You Can Call Me HOPPA!

Gammy-Goose

"*My daughter's name is* Gabrielle *and within weeks of her birth, my mom had given her the nick name, Gabby Goose. When we started talking about what my mom wanted her grandparent name to be, we couldn't resist dubbing her* **Gammy Goose**. *They both love being the 'geese' and it's really been a cute bond between the two of them.*"

– Cammie G., Austin, TX

Doc

Doodad

DubDub

Duke

Fancy

Fifi Foxy

G-Daddy

G-Diddy

Glamma

"*My mother-in-law* is an amateur actress in a local theatre company in our town. She is wonderfully dramatic and is always dressed to the nines. When we had our son, she started searching for a name other than Grandma. She read in a magazine that a very famous Hollywood actress had decided to be called **Glamma**, and none of us could think of anything that suited her more perfectly!"

– Anonymous

Gibby

Gigi

Gin-Gin

G-ma

G-mama

G-mere

G-pa

G-papa

You Can Call Me HOPPA!

Granddaddeo

"When I was a teenager, I started calling my dad 'Daddeo'. It's been what I've called him ever since, and he thought it would be fun if we could keep up the tradition by having our daughter call him Granddaddeo."

— Tracy W., Phoenix, AZ

G-pere
GrahmCrackers
Grammbo
Grammie/Grammy

Grampoo
Gramps
Grams
Gramsie

Grand-dude

"*My father-in-law* is an avid surfer and a total beach bum. He decided that he was too hip for a standard name and opted for *Grand-dude*. He and my son both love it and it's a great conversation starter."

– Janelle B., Encinitas, CA

Gran

Grananna

Grandbuddy

Grandee

Grandma Sunshine

Grandmamy

Grandmomma

Grandmommie

Grand-moo

Grandnan

Grandy

Granlady

Granma Goddess

Granmum

Granna

Grannie Ho

Grea

Grumps

Guapo

"*My mom re-married* when my daughter was young. *When my daughter met her new step-grandfather for the first time, this innocent little 4 year-old looked up at me and said 'Mama he's handsome like a prince'. We all thought it was hilarous and our Mexican-American family couldn't help but interpret this statement as cause for him to be forever called* Guapo *(Spanish for handsome).* **"**

– Maria R., Albuquerque, NM

Ha

Happy

Honey

Jazzie

Lollie

LuLu

Ma'Dear

Mamananna

KO

"*We had always called** my mom's parents Big Wal and Wal (which was a nickname a lot of people called them because their last name was Wallace). My mom's family had always called her KO (Carol) and so, I asked my mom if she liked KO and she loved it. She loved that it was original and that I wanted to do something similar to what we called her mom. So, she is now KO to all three of her grandchildren.***"*

– Megan F., Pittsburgh, PA

Mamie

MammaLamma

Manman

Meemo

Memaw/Me-ma

Memom/Me-Mom

Mimi

Mo Mo

Tootsie

"*When my husband* was little, his mom's favorite movie was Tootsie. Apparently she was pretty obsessed with it and his dad started calling her Tootsie as a nickname. My daughter started calling her Gramma at first, but as she got older she thought it was so funny that G-paw called her *Tootsie*, so she decided she would call Gramma 'Tootsie' too. It stuck and now we all refer to her that way!"

– Monica H., Burbank, CA

Mommom

Momsie

Mumma

Muncee

Nanma

Nanoo

Ninny

Nona

Nonie

Nonna

Nonnie

NuNu

Pal

Papoo/Papu

Pappy

Paw/Pa

Wicky

My dad re-married when I was in college. Because his wife is a really great person with a good sense of humor, it was easy for my brother and I to tease her and refer to her as our 'wicked step-mother'. When I had my first child, their first grandchild, we were torn about what she should be called. One afternoon she announced that she thought my son should call her *Wicky*, short for 'wicked step-grandmother'! We think it's the cutest name ever!

– Mandy R., St. Paul, MN

Pawpee

PeePaw

Pepa

Pe-Pop

Pop

PoPo

Poppa

Poppers

Poppie

Popple

PopPop

Popsie

Queenie

Sir

Tata

Tiger

Out of the Mouths of Babes

Those early words uttered by babies create some of the most special memories. Many of us remember our child's first words, and how his early attempts at 'ball' sounded more like the sound a sheep makes, and the animal that says 'ruff ruff' was affectionately known as a 'gog'. And so it goes for grandparent names… traditional grandparent names are especially difficult for little mouths to say and the result of attempts at these names is often more wonderful and endearing than anything our adult brains could have conjured. This collection of names developed by children illustrates that there are clear patterns of sound that are much easier for babies to pronounce. If you select a name with one or two syllables made up of simple sounds, it is much more likely that your grandchildren will be able to say your name sooner – a milestone to which many grandparents look forward. If you choose a name from one of the other lists, be prepared to have your mind promptly changed when your grandchild utters their own iteration of that name for the first time and it instantly melts your heart.

Bamboo

"*My granddaughter tried* so hard to say Grandma and at first it came out as a whole bunch of sounds we couldn't really identify. After a few weeks, it became as clear as day and it sounded exactly like *Bamboo*. I immediately loved it and requested that we never try to correct her again. I'm now Bamboo to all 6 grandchildren."

– Sally R., Detroit, MI

Abi-Gabi	Adda
Ami	Amma
Amma	Aya
Ammo	Baba

You Can Call Me HOPPA!

Banana

"*My mom was planning* to be called Nana just like her mom. One of my son's first words had been banana so we figured he should be able to say Nana easily. When we started trying to get him to say Nana, he giggled every time and sort of defiantly said 'banana'. It became a little family joke and my mom ended up falling in love with it and has been *Banana* ever since."

– Sara T., St. Louis, MO

Badda

Bampie

Bagoo

Bamps

Bama

Bapa

Bamaw

Bapaw

Big Joe

"My grandkids call me Big Joe. When my grandson learned the word "big", everything was big for awhile. During that time he called his other granddad Big Jim and his parents thought that was pretty cute, so he became Big Jim and I'm Big Joe.*"*

– Joe P., Newport, CA

Baw
Bea Bea
Beeps
Beerma

Beerpa
BeMa
BePa
Bobaloo

You Can Call Me HOPPA!

Boo

"When my first grandchild was very young I used to love to make her giggle with games of peek-a-boo. One day I arrived at her house and when she saw me she said Boo and began to call me that from then on! Now I'm Boo and I love it!"

– Meg D., Columbia, SC

Bompa

Booma

Boompa

Boops

Boowa

Bopee

Boppa

Bops

BopBop

" *I had decided I wanted to be called Pop Pop. When my granddaughter was a baby we tried to get her to say it but it always came out as BopBop. The cutest part was that when she said BopBop she would bend her knees and do this little bounce-like dance. How could I resist. She's 8 now and she doesn't do the dance but I'm still her BopBop.* **"**

– Graham S., Albany, NY

Budna   Buppa
Bumpa   Chippy
Bumpy   Damma
Bunny   Dappy

You Can Call Me HOPPA!

Cheap

My dad had decided he wanted his grandparent name to be Chief. We thought it was funny and we tried to get my sister's son, the first grandchild, to say it. When we finally did, it came out quite clearly as **Cheap**. It was so hilarious and so fitting that we convinced him to keep it.

— Jessica W., Phoenix, AZ

Farnarner

Gaga

Gaka

Gam/Gammie

Gani

Gankie

Geeda

Gempa

Giu-Giu

"*My mother in law*, now known as *GiuGiu*, took the first sound our son was saying and started calling herself that! She was very particular about having a special name and our kids will be her only grandkids. They still call her that years later."

– Stephanie L., Buckeye, AZ

Nana Bama

"*I grew up in Tuscaloosa, Alabama* and both of my parents went to college in Alabama. No one is a bigger Alabama sports fan than my mom. One afternoon we were visiting and were watching an Alabama v. Auburn footbal game. My mom was going crazy and cheering 'Go Bama' throughout the game. Toward the end of the game, my two year old son, who had called her Nana before that day, suddently shouted out *Nana Bama!* Needless to say, she loved it!"

– Ashley L., Birmingham, AL

Gig

Giggy

Ginga

Ging-ging

Goggie

Gogi

Gom

Gommy

Gonga

Gop

Grad

Grandy

Granin

Gree

Gubby

Gumpa

Popeye

"*My dad's dad* wanted to be known as Papa. I was a kid in the 70's when the Popeye cartoon was big, and for years I thought everyone was calling him *Popeye* so I did the same. Nobody corrected me until it was so solidified as his name that it couldn't be changed. He loved it. When we had our first baby, my dad didn't hesitate to tell us that he definitely wanted to carry on the Popeye name."

– Darren K., Atlanta, GA

You Can Call Me HOPPA!

Guppy   Papaya

Ho Ho   Pinta

JaJa   Ranny

Jan Ma   Yo

LaLa   Yammy

Maga   Yamps

Oowi-Oowi   Yummy

Pah-jaw   Yumpa

We would love to hear all about the Grandparent Name you or your little loved ones have chosen. Please visit us at CallMeHoppa.com to share the tale of how you or your grandchildren arrived at your new title. You may find your story in the next edition of You Can Call Me Hoppa!

You Can Call Me

The
Grandparent
Name Family Tree

Grandparents hold special places in our hearts and provide us with wonderful memories and stories. This page is included to allow you to chronicle the grandparent names in your heritage in one beautiful Grandparent Name Family Tree.

You Can Call Me

You Can Call Me

The co-founder of the **Southwest Autism Research and Resource Center (SARRC)** *has been a colleague of mine for many years, and I have seen SARRC touch the lives of thousands of families impacted by the heartbreaking mysteries of autism spectrum disorders (ASDs). Today 1 in 150 children are affected by an ASD – each of those children have parents and grandparents who are caring for them daily and are desperate for answers, treatments, a cure... The title of this book is* **"You Can Call Me Hoppa!"** *In many cases of ASD, children are unable to master the spoken word as autism impairs a child's expressive and receptive communication skills. Parents and grandparents hope each day to hear their child's voice engaged in some meaningful form of communication. Many only dream that they will hear their child call them Mom, Dad, Grandma or Grandpa. A portion of the proceeds from the sale of this book will be donated to SARRC as our small way of supporting the critical mission of this incredible organization. We hope our contribution allows the millions of families affected by ASDs to get even one step closer to the answers they so desperately seek.*

– Author, Lauren Charpio

The Southwest Autism Research & Resource Center (SARRC) is a nonprofit organization, based in Phoenix, Arizona, dedicated to research, education and resources for individuals with autism spectrum disorders (ASDs) and their families. SARRC undertakes self-directed research, serves as a satellite site for national and international projects, and provides up-to-date information, training and assistance to families and professionals about autism. Through integrative research, educational outreach, model programs and collaborative initiatives, SARRC sets forth, promotes and facilitates best practices for early intervention and the long-term care of individuals with ASDs.

Autism is a complex neurobiological disorder that interferes with normal development in language, social interaction and behavior. The incidence of ASDs has exploded in the past two decades and given autism the undesired ranking as the most prevalent childhood developmental disorder in the U.S. While there is no known cause, and worse yet, no cure, we do know that autism is likely the product of genetics and environmental factors. SARRC continues to advance its research by building collaborative alliances with respected scientists and institutions in Arizona, across the country and around the world.

Volunteers are the power behind nonprofit organizations like SARRC and SARRC's Grandparent Support Group leads the way with 350 dedicated members. There is never a job too big or too small for these amazing voluneers who are committed to making a difference in the lives of their children and grandchildren. They are among the millions of grandparents today who long for those precious words of acknowledgement from their grandchildren. Any words will do. "You Can Call Me Hoppa" offers many wonderful ideas and places to start.

To learn more about SARRC and autism spectrum disorders, please visit www.autismcenter.org.

About the Author

Lauren Charpio is a working mother of two living in Phoenix, Arizona. After having spent many years focused on collecting degrees and building a career, one evening Lauren hopped aboard a Southwest airplane and met her now husband, Casey, in row 15. Lauren became mom to bubbly Brooke in 2003 and Cooper the still-bald bruiser in 2006 – simultaneously creating two sets of doting first-time grandparents. Lauren and her family are blessed to have both sets of grandparents nearby. Grammie and Hoppa live a short trek north on a Ranch populated by horses, ponies and dogs. And PawPaw and Gramma live minutes from the best play area and carousel in town.